FIG

FAITH IN

GOD

Lisa Driver-Crummy and
Belinda Driver-McCain

AuthorHouse™
1663 Liberty Drive
Bloomington, IN 47403
www.authorhouse.com
Phone: 1 (800) 839-8640

Published by AuthorHouse 02/23/2019

ISBN: 978-1-5462-7613-5 (sc)
ISBN: 978-1-5462-7614-2 (e)

Library of Congress Control Number: 2019902277

Print information available on the last page.

Scripture taken from The Holy Bible, King James Version. Public Domain
References: Believer's Bible Commentary by William MacDonald

This book is printed on acid-free paper.

authorHOUSE®

CONTENTS

ACKNOWLEDGMENTS

We thank Jesus Christ for giving us the victory through all our trials, because He paid it in full at the Cross. We thank God the Father for strengthening our faith in Him. We thank the Holy Spirit for comforting us in our trials. We thank God for our families and friends. We thank Earline Moore for her continuing prayers. We thank Apostle Michael Lock and Prophetess Jennie Lock for their prayers, encouragements, and support. Also, we thank Apostle John Sawyerr for his prayers and support.

INTRODUCTION

In the book of (Mark 11:23), we find that Jesus taught us that our faith is released through our words and that our faith-filled words can move mountains. There is absolutely nothing too hard for God and nothing impossible to those who believe. Your faith is the key to seeing that the miracles and breakthroughs will happen according to the Bible. God's Word says whatever we ask in prayer, believe, and we will receive. (Matthew 21:22) In the book of (Romans 10:8), teaches us that the Word is near us.

The Word is in our heart and mouth, because they are connected. The Word of God in our heart will come through our mouth and faith in our heart will be released through our mouth. Once it is released, we can be assured that it will produce what we say. The Word of God tells us in (Jeremiah 1:12), that God watches over His Word to perform it! In (Jeremiah 33:3), encourages us to call upon the Lord, for He has promised to show us those great and mighty things we know not.

Our faith in Jesus Christ and what He did at the Cross must be proven genuine before we can operate in it. When we placed our faith in Jesus Christ, what He did on the Cross at Calvary. He suffered and died in our place, so that we wouldn't have to face the judgment of God for our sins. Then the Holy Spirit can work through us. (Ephesians 2:10)

Personal salvation is by faith in Jesus Christ which He shed His innocent blood on the Cross for the remission of our sins for all who believe. Salvation is the gift of eternal life by the grace of God apart from work. Not by works of righteousness that we have done, but it is a gift from God. (Titus 3:5-7 and Ephesians 2:8-9)

To live by strong faith is to endure trials and hardships in life. We are to be steadfast and unmovable in the Lord. (1 Corinthians 15:57-58)

We are to hold on to our faith and persevere no matter what comes our way. We are to have true confidence in God and certainty of God's promises. We are to have sure faith in God, Jesus Christ, and what He did at the Cross. Having firm faith in the Lord can remove mountains out of our way and nothing shall be impossible unto us. (Matthew 17:20)

PURPOSE

The purpose of this book, "Faith In God" is to help stir up the Believers' faith in God and to trust God in everything. This dynamic book will help the body of Jesus Christ learn that when we confess the Word of God, we build ourselves up in faith and discover that our faith can indeed move mountains. This will offer ways to build up faith in God, trust in God, and to live a victorious life in God by faith in God the father, God the Lord Jesus Christ, and God the Holy Spirit.

The devil wants you to doubt God. He doesn't want you to believe God's Holy Word. He wants to steal your faith, joy, peace, happiness, and stop your blessings from God. The blessings can be so close or right before your eyes, but you cannot see it because of distraction from the devil, such as life, family, friends, and focusing on your circumstances. But, we must keep our eyes on the Lord, have faith and trust in Him no matter what the devil throws our way. We want Believers to recognize what is from God and what is from the devil. When we keep our faith in God, we can experience love, joy, peace, happiness, healing, and prosperity. But if we doubt Him, we might experience hatred, misery, war, bitterness, sickness, and poverty, which is all from the devil.

We are to constantly have faith in God without wavery. Not changing because of our circumstances in life. We trust God because of everything is going great, but as soon as something happens or a situation that you cannot control, you start doubting God. But, this is the time to trust Him and not doubt, to praise Him and not to be angry with Him, to bless His Holy Name and not to accuse Him, and to thank Him for what He has already done.

Our prayer is that this book will be a blessing to those who read it, and that their faith would be increased daily in the God kind of faith. We pray that the Holy Spirit will reveal to Believers what they need to live and to grow faithful in God. Jesus is the author and finisher of our faith. (Hebrews 12:2)

This book can be utilized for group studies, group discussions, and as a teaching manual in churches.

FOREWORD

"This book, "Faith in God" is a testament of Elder Lisa Crummy and Rev. Belinda McCain total trust in God to walk by faith and not by sight. Their faith, trust, and humbleness are just a few of the many gifts that the Lord has blessed them with.

It is a refreshing reminder to always be prepared for spiritual warfare. They are truly an inspiration sent by the Lord to remind us to always keep the faith as well as putting on the whole armor of God daily. It reminds us to always stay true to the promises of God and never doubt.

This book will empower and encourage you to keep the faith in the Lord. It will enlighten your spiritual eyes about your personal relationship, walk, and belief in Jesus Christ and what He did at the Cross.

It will remind you to stand on God's Word and to keep the faith in God; no matter how life might seem difficult, no matter how it seems like nothing is working in your favor, or no matter how you don't understand His plan for your life."

Apostle Michael A. Lock & Prophetess Jennie Lock
Senior Pastor, We Are One In The Spirit World Outreach Ministries,
Greenville, SC

FAITH IN GOD

Faith in God is dead to doubts and blind to impossibilities. "We know that all things are possible through God." (Matthew 19:26) Having faith, we know nothing but success. Faith works! The Word of God works! The Blood of Jesus works! The Love of God works! We are to put our faith, hope, and trust in God.

Faith in God is believing that if God said it in His Word, it is true. "Faith is the substance of things hoped for, the evidence of things not seen." (Hebrews 11:1) Faith is not based on our physical eyesight, but on the Word of God. Faith is always active and trusting in God's faithfulness. Faith is a commitment to God from our action of both heart and mind.

Faith in God is essential for salvation to believe and confess with our mouth the Lord Jesus. (Romans 10:9-10) Faith in God helps us face the pressure of every day living and helps us find the strength to endure hardships. Our faith is in God's strength and His promises. Our faith depends upon the factual history of the life, death, and resurrection of Jesus.

Faith in God is believing that you have already received the promises of God, so you hold on to them. We are to place our faith in Jesus Christ and accept the finished work what He did at the Cross. Jesus Christ is coming back one day, and we are to be ready at all time! "Without faith, it is impossible to please God." (Hebrews 11:6)

Put On The Whole Armor Of God
(Ephesians 6:14-18)

ARMOR	AFFIRMATION	PLEDGE
Loins girt about with truth	Jesus is my truth.	"Jesus is the way, the truth, and the life." (John 14:6)
Breastplate of righteousness	Jesus is my righteousness.	"That we might be made The righteousness of God in Him." (2 Corin.5:21)
Feet shod with preparation of the gospel of peace	Jesus is my readiness.	"I can do all things through Christ Jesus which gives me the strength." (Phil. 4:13)
The shield of faith	Jesus is my faith.	"Jesus is the author and finisher of my faith." (Hebrews 12:2)
The helmet of salvation	Jesus is my salvation.	"Jesus became the author of eternal salvation unto all them that obey Him." (Hebrews 5:9)
The sword of the Spirit, which is the Word of God.	Jesus is my living Word.	"In the beginning was the Word, and the Word was with God, and the Word was God." (John 1:1)
Praying always with all prayer and supplication in the Spirit.	Jesus is my baptizer in the Spirit.	"He shall baptize you with The Holy Ghost, and with Fire." (Matthew 3:11)

Keypoints:

How Does A Believer Put On The Whole Armor of God?

- By faith in Jesus Christ, we are to put on the whole armor of God by believing and declaring faith in God's promises.

- By faith in Jesus Christ, we put off the works of the old man and to put on works the new man.

- By faith in Jesus Christ, we live a victorious life filled with the Spirit of God and to stand on the provision what Jesus Christ paid in full at the Cross.

- **Armor Of God: Shield Of Faith:**

  (1) Trust
  (2) Hope
  (3) Protection
  (4) Believing

- You dress in the armor of God by putting on the armor of light, our Lord and Savior Jesus Christ? Have you placed your faith only in God, Jesus Christ and what Jesus accomplished on the Cross at Calvary?

SESSION 1

What Is Faith?

"Faith is the substance of things hoped for, the evidence of things not seen." (Hebrews 11:1)

Faith is a spiritual walk that you should hear, see, feel, walk, and talk through your spiritual senses.

You hope and believe for the things that you cannot see, but it is as real as if you already have them. Faith provides unshakable evidence of things unseen, it makes the invisible seen comes to reality.

The spiritual blessings for Christians are true and real, because we have confidence in the trustworthiness of God.

Keypoints:

- Faith in God is the key that gives you the substance of things hoped for in life.

- Faith in God is the key that gives you the contentment of daily living.

- Faith in God is the key confidence that gives you the assurance that your life is secured with the Holy Spirit.

- Faith in God is the key that makes impossibilities come to reality and possibilities by looking to God alone and standing on His Word and promises.

- Faith is belief and trust in God. Faith in Jesus Christ is essential for salvation.

- Faith should always be active in trusting God.

- Faith is believing from the heart and a commitment of both heart and mind.

- Faith is confidence in the trustworthiness of God.

- If our faith is in the Lord, our faith joins us to God and unbelief separates us from God. If you have unbelief in your heart, you don't trust what God can do.

- There is nothing impossible for God and it will not be impossible for an individual who grasps the principle that Jehovah God is our source. But, we must keep our eyes on Him and place our faith and trust in Him.

↪ **We are to be steadfast by having a firm faith in God.**

↪ **We should live, walk, and talk by faith in God.**

↪ **Do you walk and see in fear and defeat or walk and see by faith?**

↪ **Do you walk and live by the Word of God, by His righteousness, and His fellowship?**

➤ **Will you choose to trust God no matter what or doubt Him?**

➤ **You can choose living a victorious life or a defeated life? The choice is yours.**

Steadfast: Devoted, dedicated, loyalty, faithful, attachment, and belief.

Trust: Belief, confidence, rely, and faith

Doubt: Distrust, uncertainty, query, and unsure

Hebrews 11:4

"By faith Abel offered unto God a more excellent sacrifice than Cain."
What does faith look like in a person's life? By faith Abel offered a superior sacrifice. Abel exhibited his faith by approaching God with the blood of an animal for the sacrifice.

Abel demonstrated the truth of salvation by grace through his faith. He brought an excellent sacrifice and his faith was in it. Cain attempted to save himself by good works. His sacrifice was one of vegetables or fruit and it was bloodless. He was a self-righteous person, and a self-righteous person hates the truth that he cannot save himself.

Keypoints:

- We are not justified by our good works, deeds, or our character.

- We cannot save ourselves, we must cast ourselves on the mercy of God. We must believe on Jesus Christ and what He did on the Cross at Calvary.

- Our daily living by faith is established upon eternal truths. Our faith as Believers should be based on the crucified, buried, and risen from the dead, our Lord and Savior, Jesus Christ.

Hebrews 11:5

By faith Enoch lived in a way that pleased God. Enoch believed in God's promises. Enoch must have received a promise from God that if he pleases God that he would go to Heaven without dying. He walked with the invisible God for three hundred and sixty-five years and then God took Him.

Keynotes:

- Enoch lived and walked in a way that pleased God. God wants to be trusted and for us to believe in His promises. We are to believe in the Creator not the creative things.

- The life of faith always pleases God. We are to place our faith in God and trust Him at His Word.

"The righteousness of God revealed from faith to faith: as it is written, the just shall live by faith." (Romans 1:17)

"No man is justified by the law in the sight of God, it is evident: for, the just shall live by faith. The law is not of faith: but, the man that doeth them shall live in them." (Galatians 3:11-12)

"The just shall live by faith: but if any man drawback, my soul shall have no pleasure in him." (Hebrews 10:38)

"For we walk by faith, not by sight." (2 Corinthians 5:7)

"As ye have therefore received Christ Jesus the Lord, so walk ye in Him: Rooted and built up in Him, and stablished in the faith, as ye have been taught, abounding therein with thanksgiving." (Colossians 2:6-7)

"Remembering without ceasing your work of faith, and labor of love, and patience of hope in our Lord Jesus Christ, in the sight of God and our Father." (1 Thessalonians 1:3)

Keynotes:

- We should live, walk, talk, hear, and see by faith.

- Living by faith, we can accomplish so much in life and be successful. But without faith in God and Jesus Christ, we will fail in life.

- Faith comes to people when they hear the preaching of the Gospel concerning the Lord Jesus Christ, which is the Word of God.

- We must hear with an open heart and mind, willing to accept the true Word of God. When you hear the truth, then they will believe.

- We should speak God's Word out loud and take authority over the power of evil by God's Word.

- Praise God out loud by faith, even if you don't feel like it.

Spiritual And Powerful Weapons Against The Enemy, Satan

Blood - The Blood of Jesus Christ

Name - Jesus

Cross - Jesus died on the Cross for all our sins

Word - The Word of God

Keynotes:

- "The Blood of Jesus Christ, the saints of God overcame him (the enemy) by the blood of the Lamb, and by the word of their testimony."

- The name of Jesus, Believers have the right to use the name of Jesus to defeat the enemy and to destroy his works and power.

- The Cross, Jesus paid it in full by His precious blood.

- The Word of God, it is a sword, the sword of the Spirit, which is the Word of God.

As A Group, Read Scriptures:

John 3:16-18   1 Peter 1:3
John 3:36   1 John 5:11-12
Hebrews 11:4-5   Revelation 12:11

How To Activate The Weapons:

Repent –   Repent is to ask the Lord to forgive you of all your sins.
              "Repent for the kingdom of Heaven is at hand." (Matthew 4:17)

Rejoice - Rejoice in Jesus' name and the victory that was won.
              "Rejoice in the Lord always: and again I say, rejoice."
              (Philippians 4:4-8)

Rebuke -   Rebuke satan, the devil, and all the wicked ones.
              "Jesus rebuked the devil; and he departed out of him: and the child
              was cured from that very hour." (Matthew 17:18)

Faith -   Faith in the Father, the Son, Jesus Christ, the Holy Spirit, and the
              Word of God.

♦ **Admit to God the Father that you need His forgiveness and salvation.**

♦ **Repent from trusting in idols gods and trusting in anything else for eternal life and trust only in Jesus Christ for salvation.**

As A Group, Read Scriptures:

Matthew 4:10
Mark 16:17-18
Hebrews 4:12
James 4:7
1 Peter 5:8-11

"For unto us was the gospel preached, as well as unto them; but the word preached did not profit them, not being mixed with faith in them that heard it." (Hebrews 4:2)

"For the preaching of the Cross is to them that perish foolishness; but unto us which are saved it is the power of God." (1 Corinthians 1:18)

"Hold fast the form of sound words, which thou hast heard of me, in faith and love which is in Christ Jesus." (2 Timothy 1:13)

"But God forbid that I should glory, save in the Cross of our Lord Jesus Christ, by whom the world is crucified unto me, and I unto the world." (Galatians 6:14)

Keynotes:

- The gospel of Jesus Christ is the power of God, to those who hear the message and accept it by faith. They are being saved and the miracle of regeneration takes place in their lives.

- There are only two types of people, those who are saved and those who are perishing. There is no in between types and you cannot serve two masters. People can love

God, place their faith in God and Jesus Christ, and accept what Jesus fulfilled at the Cross or they can despise Him, place their faith in idol gods and lose their soul.

- If a Believer is living under the law and not accepting what Jesus Christ accomplished on the Cross, it will profit him nothing. A person cannot have it two ways, grace and law. What Jesus Christ did for us on the Cross, that is the grace of God. True faith works by love, and we are to love God with all our heart, all our soul, all our strength, all our mind.

- The world cannot satisfy Believers and they have lost interest in the pleasures that the world has to offer them. Only Jesus Christ can completely satisfy Believers, and we can boast about what He accomplished on the Cross for our sins.

- If you are not receiving from God, you must put your faith from your heart into action and exercise your faith by believing every Word of God.

- Sanctification is by faith in Jesus Christ and what He accomplished at the Cross for all humankind.

- By exercising your faith from your heart, an example:

  - "I know for sure that I am already healed by the power of God."

➤ **How will you use your freedom? To serve God or to serve the devil?**

➤ **How will you live your new life under Bondage or Freedom in Jesus Christ?**

Lisa Driver-Crummy and Belinda Driver-McCain

<u>As A Group, Read Scriptures:</u>

Isaiah 53:5
John 6:47
Galatians 2:16

Galatians 2:20
1 Peter 2:24
1 Peter 3:18-22

SESSION 2

Why Is Faith Important?

"Without faith it is impossible to please Him, for he that cometh to God must believe that He is, and that He is a rewarder of them that diligently seek Him." (Hebrews 11:6)

A person refuses to believe God, he or she is calling God a liar. "He that believeth not God hath made Him a liar; because he believeth not the record that God gave of His Son." (1 John 5:10)

<u>Keynotes</u>:

- When we pray for something according to God's will, we must have the faith to know that He will answer our prayers. We must trust what answers He gives us according to His Word and the Holy Spirit.

- We are to believe by faith apart from what we can see with our physical eyes. Faith in God is walking in love, joy, and peace, not doubting but believing everything that God said in His Word.

- We are to look at things through the spiritual eyes of faith. We will only succeed in overcoming this world with the help of our Lord and Savior, Jesus Christ, and the Holy Spirit. Therefore, let us walk, talk, see, hear, and believe by faith in God, Jesus Christ, and the Holy Spirit.

- We are to keep the faith in God, Jesus Christ, and what He accomplished at the Cross. Jesus Christ paid it in full at the Cross for all our sins.

→ **Satan is always trying to get people to doubt God, lose faith, and hope.**

→ **Are you going to believe the lies of satan when he wants you to doubt the existence of God or believe that God does exist and that He is faithful?**

→ **To have Faith in God, we must believe that He does exist and that He is a rewarder.**

→ **Having faith in God, should move us to action and to prove our faith by living in a way that pleases Him.**

→ **What kind of fruit do you have in your daily living?**

Fruits Of Your Faith In God Will Show In Your Daily Living:

- Fruit of love

- Fruit of joy

- Fruit of peace

- Fruit of longsuffering

- Fruit of gentleness

- Fruit of goodness

- Fruit of excellent

- Fruit of righteousness

The Fruit Of The Spirit:

- Fruit of your faith

- Fruit of your hands

- Fruit of your mouth

- Fruit of your mind

As A Group, Read Scriptures:

Matthew 22:37
1 Corinthians 15:58
2 Corinthians 5:19
James 2:20, 26
1 Peter 5:7

SESSION 3

How Can Faith Be Tested?

"By faith Noah, being warned of God of things not seen as yet, moved with fear, prepared an ark to the saving of his house; by the which he condemned the world, and became heir of the righteousness which is by faith."

By faith Noah obeyed divined warning from God that He was going to destroy the world with a flood, he feared God, and built a humongous ark to save his household.
Human race had never experience a flood on the earth, and they might not have ever seen rainfall before the flood.

"Where is the promise of His coming?..............................But the day of the Lord will come as a thief in the night; in the which the Heavens shall pass away with a great noise, and the elements shall melt with fervent heat, the earth also and the works that are therein shall be burned up." (2 Peter 3:4-10)

Keynotes:

- Noah believed God and his household was saved, but the world was condemned. The world did not believe and was destroyed by the flood.

- The next time, it won't be by flood, but by fire, both the earth and the works that are in it will be burned up. We are to be ready at all time and expecting The Lord to come back at any time. We are to believe in His Word and trust Him that He cannot lie. **He is coming back one day!**

"By faith Abraham, when he was called to go out into a place which he should after to receive for an inheritance, obeyed; and he went out, not knowing where he was going. By faith he sojourned in the land of promise, as in a strange country. He looked for a city which hath foundations, whose builder and maker is God." (Hebrews 11: 8-10)

"By faith Sarah received strength to conceive seed, and delivered a child named Isaac, when she was past age, because she judged Him faithful Who had promised." (Hebrews 11:11)

Keynotes:

- The walk of faith gives the impression to others that we are being imprudent. But we who know God, we can trust Him to lead us and guide us on the path that He wants us to be on. We are not to have our heart set on earthly or material things, but on Eternity.

- Faith is believing that what God said in His Word is true. Faith means trusting in God, even if we cannot see or understand everything that He said in His Word.

- Faith that have not been tried, maybe weak faith. Trial of your faith comes to make you stronger.

- "By faith Abraham, when he was tried, offered up Isaac; and he that had received the promises offered up his only begotten son." (Hebrews 11:17)

- "By faith Joseph, when he died,………. He gave commandment concerning his bones." (Hebrews 11:22)

♦ Joseph was the most loved son of Jacob. Jacob gave him a coat with many colors. The brothers sold him into slavery to the Midianites, and they took him to Egypt and sold him to Potiphar. The Lord enables Joseph to find favor with Potiphar and the keeper of the prison.

♦ "When his brethren saw that their father loved him more than all his brethren, they hated him, and could not speak peaceably unto him. Joseph dreamed a dream, and told it to his brethren, and they hated him more." (Genesis 37:4-5)

♦ "By faith Moses, when he was born, was hid three months of his parents, because they saw he was a proper child." (Hebrews 11:23)

Keynotes:

- Abraham did not waver at the promises of God through unbelief. He was stronger in faith and he was convinced that what God had promised He was able to perform. God never intended for Abraham to slay Isaac, but his faith was tested and was found to be genuine.

- Joseph suffered greatly, but God used his brothers' sinful deeds to save his family from the famine. What the enemies intended for evil, God used it for his good and to save their families. He forgave his brothers and took care of them and their families.

- By faith Joseph expressed his confidence that God would bring the people of Israel out of Egypt.

- By faith Moses forsake the luxury of Egypt's palace, he obeyed and feared God. Moses' faith helped him to see being loyalty to God and the love for His people would be more valued in eternity than the worthless wealth of Pharaoh and the treasures of Egypt.

- Moses' parents knew that he was a child of destiny and was chosen by God for a special work. Their faith that God's purposes would be worked out, it gave them the courage to disobey the king's command, and they hide Moses for three months.

James 2:14-26

(v.14)   "What doth it profits, my brethren, though a man say he hath faith, and have not works? Can faith save him?"

(v.17)   "Even so faith, if it hath not works, is dead, being alone."

(v.18)   "Yea, a man may say, thou hast faith and I have works: shew me thy faith without thy works, and I will shew thee my faith by my works."

(v.19)   "Thou believes that there is one God; thou does well: the devils also believe, and tremble."

(v.20)   "But wilt thou know, O vain man, that faith without works is dead?"

(v.21)   "Was not Abraham our father justified by works, when he had offered Isaac his son upon the altar?"

(v.22)   "See thou how faith wrought with his works, and by works was faith made perfect?"

(v.23)   "Abraham believed God, and it was imputed unto him for righteousness: and he was called the friend of God."

(v.24)   "Ye see then how that by works a man is justified, and not by faith only."

(v.26)   "For as the body without the spirit is dead, so faith without works is dead also."

➤ <u>**Faith Without Works:**</u>

- Is dead
- Is useless

<u>Keynotes:</u>

- It is heresy, if people believe that they are saved by faith plus works. They are saying in so many words that the Lord Jesus as Savior, is not enough. They try to add to Jesus' redemptive work by their own deeds of devotion and charity. But, we are justified by grace. (Romans 3:24)

    - "Being justified by faith, we have peace with God through our Lord Jesus Christ." (Romans 5:1)

- Having faith and accepting the free gift is our response to God's grace.

    - "Being now justified by His blood, we shall be saved from wrath through Him." (Romans 5:9)

- The debt of sin was met by the precious blood of Jesus Christ. Jesus paid it in full by His blood at the Cross in order to secure our justification. God can justify ungodly sinners because of Jesus Christ shedding His precious innocent blood, therefore, a righteous satisfaction has been paid in full. "It is God that justifies." (Romans 8:33)

- "Jesus was raised again for our justification." (Roman 4:25)

- The power that raised Jesus Christ from the dead. Jesus resurrection proves that God was satisfied. The blood is the price in which Jesus Christ our Savior had to pay, but God's grace is the principle upon which He justifies.

- Having faith in God and Jesus Christ and what He paid in full on the Cross, faith is the means in which we receive it.

- If people believe that they were saved by faith plus works, then there would be two saviors, Jesus and themselves. But, we only have one and the only Savior, Jesus Christ. When a person has faith, it is demonstrated by his life and the fruits that he bears.

➤ **How has the Lord tested you and did He miraculously provide a way of escape?**

➤ **Why was Abraham and Sarah struggling with the promises of God?**

➤ **Why do you think that God tested Abraham's faith, although he had shown that he had believed and had faith in God?**

➤ **How has someone done you wrong, and was it easy to forgive that person?**

➤ **In what ways does God demand for Christians to be set apart for Him in today time?**

As A Group, Read Scriptures:

Genesis 12; 15; 17

Genesis 37; 39

Genesis 46; 47; 50

Romans 2:29

1 Corinthians 3:11-21

1 Thessalonians 1:2-4

James 2:17-18

1 Peter 1:3-9

SESSION 4

Where Is Your Faith?

Daniel 3:1-28

(v.1) "Nebuchadnezzar the king made an idolatrous image of gold."

(v.12) "There are certain Jews whom thou hast set over the affairs of the province of Babylon, Shadrach, Meshach, and Abednego;.......They serve not thy gods, nor worship the golden image which thou hast set up."

(v.17) "If it be so, our God Whom we serve is able to deliver us from the burning fiery furnace, and He will deliver us out of thine hand, O king."

(v.25) "….I see four men loose, walking in the midst of the fire, and they have no hurt; and the form of the fourth is like the Son of God."

(v.28) "Nebuchadnezzar spoke, and said, blessed be the God of Shadrach, Meshach, and Abednego, who hath sent His angel, and delivered His servants that trusted in Him,…that they might not serve nor worship any god, except their own God."

Keynotes:

- Shadrach, Meshach, and Abednego were faithful Jews to God, they refused to worship the idol image of gold and they were reported by Chaldeans to the king. The three Hebrew boys were unharmed.

  Their faithfulness and confidence in God's deliverance was magnificent. They stayed true to their belief in the Lord.

- The Lord will either deliver us out of trouble or He will be with us in our trouble. In our afflictions and trials, we will succeed in achieving God's purposes for our lives and set us free from those things that might have us bind.

Daniel 6:16, 23

(v.16) "The king commanded to have Daniel cast into the den of lions. The king said unto Daniel, Thy God Whom thou serve continually, He will deliver thee."

(v.23) "Daniel was taken up out of the den, and no manner of hurt was found upon him, because he believed in His God."

Keynotes:

- Daniel stayed steadfast in his faith to God. He kept his high standard of faith and morals.

- Daniel was unharmed by the lions. He was delivered because he had faith in God.

- Daniel's accusers were cast into the lions' den and were devoured.

- The result was that king Darius issued a decree to all the people, nations, and languages by honoring the God of Daniel.

→ **We are to put actions with our faith, not bound to man, but to trust God all the way.**

→ **Are you going to trust God or trust man?**

→ **Are you a strong or a weak Christian?**

A Strong Christian:

- Strong faith in God

- Strong faith in Jesus Christ

- Strong belief in God and Jesus Christ

- Strong trust in God and Jesus Christ

A Weak Christian:

- Worry

- Doubt and speak negative

- Lack of trust

- Fear man

Keynotes:

- Faith is believing that God cannot lie.

- Faith is trusting that God cannot fail.

- Faith is believing and trusting God at His Word (the Bible).

- Faith is hoping that we will receive the promises of God.

- Faith is knowing that we have confidence in God, that He will send Jesus back to take us home (Heaven).

- Faith is a daily lifestyle that you must walk, talk, see, and hear by faith in God.

As A Group, Read Scriptures:

Numbers 23:19
Deuteronomy 31:6
Daniel 3
Daniel 6
Luke 18:8

SESSION 5

Holding On To Your Faith

♦ "How long wilt thou forget me, O Lord? forever? How long wilt thou hide thy face from me? But I have trusted in thy mercy; my heart shall rejoice in thy salvation." (Psalm 13:1,5)

♦ David felt isolation from God, when he was running for his life from Saul. He thought that God was not with him during his intense trials.

♦ David was a man after God's own heart.

♦ "Fight the good fight of faith, lay hold on eternal life, whereunto thou art also called, and hast professed a good profession before many witnesses." (1Timothy 6:12)

➢ **The word fight does not mean to combat, but rather to contend. The good fight is the Christian faith and the race connected with it, to stay in the race and to hold on to our faith and eternal life.**

♦ "Naomi's sons took wives of the women of Moab; the name of the one was Orpah, and the name of the other Ruth; and they dwelled there about ten years." (Ruth 1:4)

♦ Ruth was married to Naomi's son. Naomi lost her husband and two sons. She decided to move back to Bethlehem in Judah. Her daughter-in-law Ruth came with her. Ruth was a Moabite woman. She was committed to Naomi and she wanted to follow the God of Israel. Boaz was a relative to Ruth's husband who had passed away, therefore, he was qualified to marry her and to continue his lineage.

♦ "Fear none of those things which thou shalt suffer: behold, the devil shall cast some of you into prison, that ye may be tried; and ye shall have tribulation ten days: be thou faithful unto death, and I will give thee a crown of life." (Revelation 2:10)

<u>Keynotes:</u>

- When we face tough times in life, we must never give up on God and our faith in Him. We are going to face trials and suffering situations in life, but we must keep our faith in God and be faithful to Him even to the point of death.

- We are to live absolutely by faith in believing, trusting in God's Word and His trustworthiness. We are not to live by feelings, circumstances, fears, symptoms, or by what other people think about us.

- We are to have full assurance of faith by the confidence in the promises of God. The confidence in God's promises will result in a heart-felt assurance, security, and to persevere through life trials.

- Satan will do anything he can to try to distract you from believing God and trusting in His promises. Paul was given a thorn in the flesh, the messenger of satan.

- The most important thing is to keep our faith and trust in God even unto the end. God's timing is perfect for our situations, but we must hold on until the end. He knows how and when to bring us out of our situations.

Two Ways To Live:

1. One way is to live by faith in God, Jesus Christ, and what Jesus Christ did at the Cross of Calvary. This is the ultimately Christian way of living and holding on to the faith. Christians faith in God is based on what we cannot see. But, Christians are convinced by faith that God is real and that He is almighty and all powerful. Also, Christians are confidence without a doubt that Jesus Christ is the Way, the Truth, and the Life. (John 14:6)

2. The other way is to live by your eyesight. If you base your life on what you can see, you intended to live a life full of disappointment.

Keynotes:

- Christians who have placed their faith in God and Jesus Christ. Christians faith should involve being committed to God's will and having confidence in His promises according to His Holy Word.

- God honors our faith, not works of an individual. An individual's life must be from the beginning to the end based on faith in God, Jesus Christ, and the finished work of Jesus Christ's sacrifice at the Cross.

- God resurrected Jesus from the dead on the third day, it showed that God accepted Jesus' death on the Cross as a payment for our sins.

➤ **List some ways faith in Jesus Christ has helped you face the pressure of daily living?**

➤ **When you trust God at His Word, you are having confidence in His integrity.**

➤ **When you place your faith in God, you will have substance.**

➤ **He is well able to perform whatever He said that He will do in His Word.**

➤ **Have you accepted God's unwavering love or believed the lies of the devil that God doesn't love you?**

As A Group, Read Scriptures:

1 Samuel 13:14; 19:18-20	Acts 13:22-24
1 Samuel 23:7-26	1 Corinthians 10:13
1 Samuel 30:6	2 Corinthians 12:7-9
John 3:16	Hebrews 12:7-11
Romans 5:8-11	Ephesians 2:8-9
Matthew 1:21	1 Peter 3:18

SESSION 6

Overcoming Faith

♦ "Whatsoever is born of God overcomes the world: and this is the victory that overcomes the world, even our faith." (1 John 5:4)

♦ "Who are kept by the power of God through faith unto salvation ready to be revealed in the last time." (1 Peter 1:5)

♦ "Receiving the end of your faith, even the salvation of your souls." (1 Peter 1:9)

Keynotes:

- Only the people who are born of God will overcome the world, because by faith, they realize that the things which are seen are temporary and the things which are not seen are eternal.

- Jesus is very strong, so when we maintain our faith in Jesus, we win, we have the victory, overcome the world, the flesh, and the devil.

➤ **The Lord is the only One, Who with the exclusive right to rule and reign in our hearts and lives.**

➤ **Jesus is the only One Who died and saved us from our sins.**

➤ **Christ is God's Anointed One Who redeemed us and has been exalted to Heaven's highest place, sits at the right hand of God's throne.**

♦ "Let us draw near with a true heart in full assurance of faith, having our hearts sprinkled from an evil conscience, and our bodies washed with pure water. Let us hold fast the profession of our faith without wavering; (for He is faithful that promised)." (Hebrews 10:22-23)

♦ "Cast not away therefore your confidence, which hath great recompense of reward. For ye have need of patience, that, after ye have done the will of God, ye might receive the promise. For yet a little while, and He that shall come will come, and will not tarry." (Hebrews 10:35-37)

♦ Believers identify themselves with Jesus Christ, by death to sin, the burial of the old life, and the resurrection to walk in newness of life in Jesus Christ. Living a Christ-like life is a testimony of our faith in Jesus and the final resurrection of the dead. Believers who believes in the teachings of Jesus Christ.

Keynotes:

1. With a true heart: Our approach should be with a sincerity heart that is a commitment to Jesus Christ.

2. In full assurance of faith: We should draw near with a heart-felt assurance of confidence in the promises of God. By having this confidence in God, it will allow us to persevere through any circumstances and trials.

3. Having our hearts sprinkled from an evil conscience: This is only by the new birth in accepting what Jesus Christ did at the Cross. We have been washed and cleansed by the precious blood of Jesus Christ.

4. Our bodies washed with pure water: Our bodies represent our lives. The pure water refers to the Holy Spirit purifying an individual's life from the defilement of sin by the Word of God. In order to enter the presence of God: sincerity, assurance, salvation, and sanctification.

5. We must be steadfast in our confession of faith and hope in Christ Jesus. Our confession of hope is a declaration of salvation. He Who promised is faithful. God's promises are reliable. He can never fail, and His promises can never fail. Our Lord and Savior, Jesus Christ will come back one day as God has promised.

➤ **Where have you placed your faith and trust, Jesus Christ the center of your Christian's faith walk or in yourself, man, family, or job?**

➤ **Have you acknowledged the Lord on your job or compromised with the world?**

➤ **Have you allowed the Lord to transformed you or have you been conformed to the world?**

As A Group, Read Scriptures:

Deuteronomy 31:6

John 3:18

James 1:6

Ephesians 2:10

Galatians 2:16-20

1 Peter 1:2-23

1 Peter 3:18-22

1 Peter 5:8

1 John 4:4; 5:1-15

Revelation 3:21

SESSION 7

The Trial of Your Faith

"The Lord gave, and the Lord hath taken away; blessed be the name of the Lord. In all this Job sinned not, nor charged God foolishly." (Job 1:21-22)

"Though He slay me, yet will I trust in Him: but I will maintain mine own ways before Him." (Job 13:15)

"He knows the way that I take: when He hath tried me, I shall come forth as gold." (Job 23:10)

♦ When Job lost his sons and daughters, his servants, his wealth, and was stricken with painful sores throughout his body. It would have been easy for Job to blame God and abandon his faith in God.

♦ He held onto his faith in God without wavering even when his life was full of sorry, pain, and agony.

1 Peter 1:2-7

(v.2) "Elect according to the foreknowledge of God the Father, through sanctification of the Spirit, unto obedience and sprinkling of the blood of Jesus Christ: Grace unto you, and peace, be multiplied."

(v.3) "Blessed be the God and Father of our Lord Jesus Christ, which according to His abundant mercy hath begotten us again unto a lively hope by the resurrection of Jesus Christ from the dead."

(v.4) "To an inheritance incorruptible, and undefiled, and that fade not away, reserved in Heaven for you."

(v.5) "Who are kept by the power of God through faith unto salvation ready to be revealed in the last time."

(v.6) "Wherein ye greatly rejoice, though now for a season, if need be, ye are in heaviness through manifold temptations."

(v.7) "The trial of your faith, being much more precious than of gold that perish, though it be tried with fire, might be found unto praise, honor, and glory at the appearing of Jesus Christ."

Keynotes:

- The genuine of faith can be proved by fire. A person who is religious might not be able to withstand the trials and sufferings of this world and might fail the test. A person who has true faith is indestructible and can undergo severe tests and trials of this world. The fire of trials and tests can prove how real your faith is in Jesus Christ.

- God will award Believers who were able to accept and withstand their tribulations with joyful praise in God although surrounded by trials and troubles.

- Trials build strength, perseverance, and lead to God's glorification.

2 Corinthians 4:16-18

(v.16) "For which cause we faint not; but though our outward man perishes, yet the inward man is renewed day by day."

(v.17) "For our light affliction, which is but for a moment, worketh for us a far more exceeding and eternal weight of glory."

(v.18) "While we look not at the things which are seen, but at the things which are not seen: for the things which are seen are temporal; but the things which are not seen are eternal."

♦ "Jesus said unto them, because of your unbelief: for verily I say unto you, if ye have faith as a grain of mustard seed, ye shall say unto this mountain, remove hence to yonder place; and it shall remove; and nothing shall be impossible unto you." (Matthew 17:20)

♦ Don't blame God for the disasters in your life and give up your faith.
God answers prayers in His own time, but He is always on time.
Although we go through afflictions, but God still has a plan for our lives and He will take care of us.

Keynotes:

- A Christian's heart becomes the home of Christ Jesus. The heart is the center of the Christian's spiritual life. We are to be rooted and grounded in love as a way of life. The life of love is a life of the love of God. It is kindness, unselfish, compassion, and meekness.

- The good fight is the Christian's faith and the race connected with it. To win in this race, you must keep your faith in Christ Jesus and lay hold on eternal life.

- If a person has faith of the size of a mustard seed which is the smallest of seeds. They could command a mountain to be cast into the sea and it will happen. True faith must be based on God's promises.

- The God kind of faith can help you to move mountains and giants out of your way. If you whole heartily follow the Lord, He will order your steps and give you the victory in every situations.

- If you have true faith in God and His Word, you don't have to fight in this battle, just stand on His Word and trust Him every step of the way.

- Faith is seeing every day through the eyes of faith. Faith is seeing through the spiritual eyes and not the physical eyes.

- The Word of God is the proof when we cannot see Him.

(1.) Turn your worries, your concerns, your failures, your heartaches, and your problems to God.

(2.) The way you live your life will demonstrate what you really believe in and where you have placed your faith in.

(3.) If you want to walk in the light, you will shine in the dark, and see the truth.

(4.) If you want to be a godly example, you will walk according to the truth.

(5.) If you want to please God, you will obey Him and love the truth. If we love Him, we must obey His Commandments.

(6.) If you want to make wise choices, you need to know the truth.

➢ **Have you affirmed your faith in God or what obstacles keeping you from having faith in God daily?**

➢ **You can choose to have faith in God and live a victorious life or you can choose to doubt Him and live a defeated life.**

↪ **Jesus Christ is the source of everything. The Cross is the mean for everything. The Holy Spirit over sees it all.**

↪ **Our salvation is received through repentance toward God and having faith toward the Lord Jesus Christ.**

↪ **We are to shine our light in this world and serve God faithfully.**

<u>The Trial Of Our Faith:</u>

Concerns a test, and it is referring to testing for trustworthiness. We all have experienced test and trials of our personal faith in the Lord.

<u>Keynote:</u>

- We must know that the fiery trial is not designed to punish us, but it is to prove our faith in the Lord and purify us.

- The most often asked question during a test or trial: "Why?"

- Job asked "Why?" sixteen times. "But He knows the way that I take: When He hath tried me, I shall come forth as gold." (Job 23:10)

- Job was confident that when the trial is over, he will "come forth as gold." The trial will make a difference in Him in many ways. He also knew that the trial had an ending and that he would be purified and more precious to God.

- The Holy Spirit reminds us that we are the children of God.
- We are secure in God's hands.
- God will never leave us.
- God will keep us in perfect peace.
- God will deliver us on time.

James 1:12

"Blessed is the man that endures temptation: for when he is tried, he shall receive the crown of life, which the Lord hath promised to them that love Him."

1 Peter 1:3-5

"Blessed be the God and Father of our Lord Jesus, which according to His abundant mercy hath begotten us again unto a lively hope by the resurrection of Jesus Christ from the dead, to an inheritance incorruptible,…..who are kept by the power of God through faith unto salvation ready to be revealed in the last time."

➤ **Why did Job's three friends come to visit him and think that he was experiencing evil?**

➤ **Do you think that Job's three friends had a good understanding of God and why Believers in the faith encounters severe suffering?**

→ When you encounter suffering, do you blame God for your suffering?

→ Have you in life felt that God was not with you or have you clearly felt God's presence in your life?

→ How has faith in God helped you overcome hardship, disappointment, depression, and anxiety?

→ Are you experiencing any trials and storms in your life today?

As A Group, Read Scriptures:

Job 1; 8

Job 15; 20; 22

Job 23;24

Job 38; 40

Job 42:7-17

Psalm 32:7; 34:4

Psalm 71

Isaiah 26:3

James 5:11-15

1 Peter 1:3-9

SESSION 8

Standing Firm In The Faith

Hebrews 3:14; 4:14; 6:11-12; 10:23

(3:14) "For we are made partakers of Christ, if we hold the beginning of our confidence steadfast."

(4:14) "Seeing then that we have a great high priest, that is passed into the Heavens, Jesus the Son of God, let us hold fast our profession."

(6:11-12) "Desire that every one of you do shew the same diligence to the full assurance of hope unto the end. That ye be not slothful, but followers of them who through faith and patience inherit the promises."

(10:23) "Let us hold fast the profession of our faith without wavering; (for He is faithful that promised)."

1Corinthians 2:5; 16:13

(2:5) "That your faith should not stand in the wisdom of men, but in the power of God."

(16:13) "Watch ye, stand fast in the faith, quit you like men, be strong."

Philippians 1:27; 4:1,13

(1:27) "Only let your conversation be as it becometh the gospel of Christ: that whether I come and see you, or else be absent, I may hear of your affairs, that ye stand fast in one spirit, with one mind striving together for the faith of the gospel."

(4:1) "Therefore, my brethren dearly beloved and longed for, my joy and crown, so stand fast in the Lord, my dearly beloved."

(4:13) "I can do all things through Christ which strengthen me."

Colossians 1:23

"If ye continue in the faith grounded and settled, and be not moved away from the hope of the gospel, which ye have heard, and which was preached to every creature which is under Heaven; where of I Paul am made a minister."

2 Thessalonians 2:15

"Therefore, brethren, stand fast, and hold the traditions which ye have been taught, whether by Word, or our epistle."

- Faith must be in active, obedience to the will of God, and accepting what Jesus Christ did at the Cross.

- No matter what the devil throws our way, we are to faithfully and boldly live, serve, and stand fast in our faith in Jesus Christ, our Lord and Savior. We are to faithfully obey the Lord Jesus Christ, our Master.

Keynotes:

How Can We Stand Firm In The Faith?

- Be stedfast in the faith of the Lord Jesus Christ, what He accomplished at the Cross, and the Word of God.

- Be devoted to the Lord.

- Be brave in the Lord.

- Be courageous.

- Be unshakeable.

- Have a sincere faith in the Lord.

Do You Hold Fast Or Waiver In Your Belief?

- We are to hold fast in our beginning confidence and to be steadfast to the end.

- We are to be rooted and grounded in the Word of God and unmovable in the Lord.

- Faith is the root of salvation and endurance is the fruit of our labor.

- Being steadfast in the faith of the Lord Jesus Christ, prove that we belong to Him and have confidence in Him.

- Place your trust, hope, and faith in God.

- Praise and glorify God for Who He is.

➢ **How has your faith in the Lord stood the test?**

➢ **How has the Gospel of Jesus Christ helped you put the bad situations that happened in your life in the proper perspective?**

➢ **How has the Lord provided for you when you stayed faithful to Him during the midst of your storms?**

<u>As A Group, Read Scriptures:</u>

Mark 11:24; 16:16
Romans 12:2
1 Corinthians 15:58
2 Corinthians 4:18
Galatians 5:5
2 Timothy 3:12
1 Thessalonians 3:7-8
James 1:2-8
1 Peter 5:9

SESSION 9

Sustaining Faith

Matthew 15:28

"Then Jesus answered and said unto her, O woman, great is thy faith: be it unto thee even as thou wilt. And her daughter was made whole from that very hour."

Matthew 21:21

"Jesus answered and said unto them, verily I say unto you, if ye have faith, and doubt not, ye shall not only do this which is done to the fig tree, but also if ye shall say unto this mountain, be thou removed, and be thou cast into the see; it shall be done."

Romans 1:17

"For therein is the righteousness of God revealed from faith to faith; as it is written, the just shall live by faith."

Romans 4:13

"For the promise, that he should be the heir of the world, was not to Abraham, or to his seed, through the law, but through the righteousness of faith."

Romans 4:21

"Being fully persuaded that, what He had promised, He was able to perform."

Romans 5:1

"Therefore, being justified by faith, we have peace with God through our Lord Jesus Christ. By Whom also we have access by faith into this grace wherein we stand and rejoice in hope of the glory of God."

Romans 10:10

"For with the heart man believeth unto righteousness; and with the mouth confession is made unto salvation."

Romans 15:13

"Now the God of hope fill you with all joy and peace in believing, that ye may abound in hope, through the power of the Holy Ghost."

2 Timothy 4:7

"I have fought a good fight, I have finished my course, I have kept the faith."

Keynotes:

- Abraham, Sarah, Isaac, and Jacob did not live to see the fulfillment of the divine promises. They did not received the possession of Canaan before their death. They did not see the fulfillment of the promise of the Messiah, Jesus. They were persuaded that God would keep His promises. They had the promises in their hearts, minds, and faith to believe that God was going to fulfill all His promises.

- Faith can lay hold of blessings at a distance by believing and trusting in God's promises.

- The stronger your faith in God, is the more fervent your desires will be in Him and not the desires of this world. The greatest act of faith was when Abraham offered up Isaac.

How To Withstand The Pressure Of Life When You Are In A Severe Storm?

- Endure in the faith of the Lord Jesus Christ
- Persevere in the faith of the Lord Jesus Christ
- Stand your ground in the faith of the Lord Jesus Christ
- Great boldness in the faith of the Lord Jesus Christ
- The Holy Spirit gives us the strength, the power, and the motivation we need in order to persevere in the faith even when life situations get unbearable.
- No time to faint, hold on to your faith.

➣ **List some ways faith in God has been the strongest:**

➣ **List some circumstances in which you were weak in your faith:**

➣ **What are some lessons in life that you have learned from past mistakes?**

As A Group, Read Scriptures:

John 1:12; 3:33-36; 11:25-26
Galatians 2:20; 3:22
1 Timothy 4:12
Titus 1:2
1 John 5:13-14

SESSION 10

Faithful Or Unfaithful When Jesus Christ Returns?

<u>Mark 13:35-37</u>

(v.35) "Watch ye therefore: for ye know not when the master of the house cometh, at even, or at midnight, or at the cockcrowing, or in the morning. **(v.36)** "Lest coming suddenly He find you sleeping."

(v.37) "And what I say unto you I say unto all, Watch."

<u>1 Timothy 6:10-21</u>

(v.10) "For the love of money is the root of all evil: which while some coveted after, they have erred from the faith, and pierced themselves through with many sorrows."

(v.11) "But thou, O man of God, flee these things; and follow after righteousness, godliness, faith, love, patience, and meekness."

(v.12) "Fight the good fight of faith, lay hold on eternal life, whereunto thou art also called, and hast professed a good profession before many witnesses."

(v.13) "I give thee charge in the sight of God, who quicken all things, and Before Pontius Pilate witnessed a good confession."

(v.14) "That thou keep this commandment without spot, unrebukable, until the appearing of our Lord Jesus Christ."

(v.15) "Which in His times He shall shew, who is the blessed and only Potentate King of kings, and Lord of lords."

(v.16) "Who only hath immortality, dwelling in the light which no man can approach unto; Whom no man hath seen, nor can see: to Whom be honor and power everlasting, Amen."

(v.17) "Charge them that are rich in this world, that they be not high minded, nor trust in uncertain riches, but in the living God, Who giveth us richly all things to enjoy."

(v.18) "That they do good, that they be rich in good works, ready to distribute, willing to communicate."

(v.19) "Laying up in store for themselves a good foundation against the time to come, that they may lay hold on eternal life."

(v.20) "O Timothy, keep that which is committed to thy trust, avoiding profane and vain babblings, and oppositions of science falsely so called."

(v.21) "Which some professing have erred concerning the faith. Grace be with thee." Amen.

Philippians 2:9-16

(v.9) "Wherefore God also hath highly exalted Him, and given Him a name which is above every name."

(v.10) "That at the name of Jesus every knee should bow, of things in Heaven, and things in earth, and things under the earth."

(v.11) "And that every tongue should confess that Jesus Christ is Lord, to the glory of God the Father."

(v.12) "Wherefore, my beloved, as ye have always obeyed, not as in my presence only, but now much more in my absence, work out your own salvation with fear and trembling."

(v.13) "For it is God which worketh in you both to will and to do of His good pleasure."

(v.14) "Do all things without murmurings and disputing."

(v.15) "That ye may be blameless and harmless, the sons of God, without rebuke, during the midst of a crooked and perverse nation, among whom ye shine as lights in the world."

(v.16) "Holding forth the word of life; that I may rejoice in the day of Christ, that I have not run in vain, neither labored in vain."

Matthew 25:23

"His Lord said unto him, Well done, good and faithful servant; thou hast been Faithful over a few things, I will make thee ruler over many things: enter thou into the joy of thy Lord."

Revelation 2:13,25-26

(v.13) "I know thy works, and where thou dwellest, even where satan's seat is: and thou hold fast my name, and hast not denied my faith, even in those days wherein Antipas was my faithful martyr, who was slain among you, where satan dwelleth."

(v.25) "But that which ye have already hold fast till I come."

(v.26) "And he that overcomes, and keeps my works unto the end, to him will I give power over the nations."

1 Corinthians 9:24-25

(v.24) "Know ye not that they which run in a race run all, but one receives the Prize? So run, that ye may obtain."

(v.25) "And every man that strive for the mastery is temperate in all things. Now they do it to obtain a corruptible crown; but we an incorruptible."

Matthew 24:50

"The Lord of that servant shall come in a day when he looks not for Him, and in an hour that He is not aware of."

Luke 17:29-30

"But the same day that Lot went out of Sodom it rained fire and brimstone from Heaven and destroyed them all. Even thus shall it be in the day when the Son of man is revealed."

2 Peter 3:10-18

"But the day of the Lord will come as a thief in the night; in the which the Heavens shall pass away with a great noise, and the elements shall melt with fervent heat, the earth also and the works that are therein shall be burned up."

Titus 2:11-13

"For the grace of God that bringeth salvation hath appeared to all men, teaching us that, denying ungodliness and worldly lusts. We should live soberly, righteously, and godly, in this present world; looking for that blessed hope, and the glorious appearing of the great God and our Savior Jesus Christ."

Keypoints:

- The day of the Lord will be great day for the final triumph over the enemy. We should earnestly desire for the coming day of the Lord.

- We should want to grow in the knowledge of the Lord by studying His Word.

- Jesus Christ is coming back, and He will reward those who have persevered in the faith and remained faithful to Him even until the end.

Faithful:

Having Faith
Fidelity
Loyalty
Devoted
Reliable
Confidence
Steadfast

→ **How can we be faithful to God?**

→ **What does faithfulness to God means?**

→ **How will you be found by Jesus, when He returns?**

- Faithful and steadfast or unfaithful and not steadfast
- Spotless and blameless or spotted and blemished

➢ **Will you be prepared or unprepared for the coming of the Lord?**

➢ **Are you a friend with the world or an enemy with God?**

<u>Would People Recognize You As A Follower Of Jesus Christ?</u>

On a scale of 1 to 10

1	2	3	4	5	6	7	8	9	10

Look like the world,
wouldn't recognize you as a
Christian.

You stand out, look and act
like a Christian.

<u>As A Group, Read Scriptures:</u>

Jeremiah 39:17-18
Hebrews 13:5
2 Peter 2:9
1 John 4: 4-7

Passport To Heaven

Will You Have The Right Passport To Heaven?

- Faith in God
- Faith in the Lord Jesus Christ and what He did on the Cross at Calvary
- Accepted Jesus Christ as Lord and Savior
- Through the blood of Jesus Christ

Will You Have The Wrong Passport To Heaven?

- Church membership
- Good works
- Only keeping the Commandments
- Being a nice person and a people pleaser

Keynotes:

- Through the blood of Jesus Christ, will grant you access to Heaven.
- The shedding of innocent blood from Jesus Christ was accepted by God, the Father.
- The credential of Jesus Christ qualified Him to die on the Cross for all our sins.
- We must accept what Jesus did at the Cross and believe that He paid it in full for all our sins.

Scripture To Read:

Romans 10:9-11

The Teacup Believer

(An Illustration Of An Individual Whose Faith Has Been Tried)

"A woman was visiting in a foreign country, she stopped in a special antique shop on her tour, because she loved to collect old things. She saw a precious Teacup in an unique glass, and she wanted it so badly. As she was touching, handling, and admiring its beauty, the Teacup suddenly spoke."

"I was not always beautiful, I was just a lump of clay in the Potter's hands." "First, he put on his wheel and spun me around so many times until I was so dizzy." "I cried, Stop!" "I cannot take this, but his answer was, Not Yet!" "Next, he took me off the wheel, patted and shaped me, then put me in a very hot oven." "I cried, Stop!" "I cannot stand this hot heat, its unbearable", "Not Yet!" he said. "Then, he took me out of the oven and started to paint me with very bright colors, but the fumes from the paint were very strong." "I cried, Stop!" "I cannot stand the terrible smell, but he answered, Not Yet!" "Afterward, he put me in another hot oven that was twice as hot as the first oven." "I screamed as loud as I could, please Stop!" "I surely cannot stand this." "Not Yet!" he said. "He stated, just a little more and then you can come out." "Finally, he took me out of the fire, and smiled." "He gave me a mirror to see myself, I cried, because I could not believe how beautiful I turned out to be." "I saw that I was the most beautiful Teacup in the world."

"I had to thank my Master Potter for taking me through the test and trial." "I could not have imagine being beautiful." "But saw myself as an ugly lump of clay." "But, He knew what was best for me." "He knew that I could endure all the test, trials, and fire in the end, and that I would turn out to be something beautiful, just like He saw me in the beginning." "Lord, I'm very glad that You allow me to go through the fire." "I have a closer walk with You, and I can be a pleasure to others who see me now." "Now, my faith was strengthened to believe that You can easily deliver me from every trials and challenging situations."

Dear Heavenly Father,

(Prayer)

"I surrender myself totally to You in faith and trust for You are the true living God. I refuse to doubt and be discouraged in the chaos that this world has to offer. Father, thank You for giving us peace in our storms of life. God take my faith to a higher level so that I can overcome every stumbling blocks, shackles, heartaches, embarrassments, poverty, and neglect. I want to rise above all negative feelings of my past that have deterrent me in life. Father, You reign forever in every circumstances and You are our source. I want my faith to be concrete in You, my God that I trust with my whole heart to lead me and guide me every step of the way to Heaven. I refuse to believe my feelings about what the enemy tries to put in my mind. I declare total victory everyday over all satanic forces that try to hinder me from the Will of God. God help me to focus and discern what is Your perfect will for my life. You are the God of all hope, love, and power. I trust You God, believe in Your promises, and stand firm on Your Holy Word, the Bible. I believe that Jesus died on the Cross at Calvary in my place, so that all my sins can be forgiven. Also, I believe that Jesus rose on the third day, so that I can have eternal life. Thank You Heavenly Father for loving me so much to make this possible through Christ Jesus! In Jesus' name, Amen!"

SESSION 1

Introducing The Study:

In this lesson, we will study what is faith, how to be steadfast, how to believe, trust, and have confidence in God no matter what the circumstances are.

♦ **Faith** is based on believing and trusting in God Who cannot lie and He keeps His promises.

♦ **Faith** is always active in believing and hoping in God.

♦ **Faith** is a commitment of both heart and mind.

♦ **Faith** leads to obedience.

♦ **Faith** in God and Jesus Christ Who provides salvation for all our sins.

- Faith is a genuine faith of a person who is committed to God and depending on the finished work of Christ's sacrifice as the only basis for forgiveness of sin and entrance into Heaven.

- Faith is a personal commitment of an individual's life to follow Jesus Christ and to be obedience to His Commandments.

- Faith is assurance that we will receive the things for which we hope for according to God's Will and His promises.

Scriptures:

John 3:16
Hebrews 11:1
Jude 1:3

SESSION 2

Introducing The Study:

In this lesson, we will study why it is essential to have faith in God. We cannot please God without faith. We cannot receive salvation without faith in God and Jesus Christ.

♦ Only faith can please God, and it proves that we have confidence in Him than relying on our own eyesight.

♦ By having faith is not only believing that God exists, but having the faith to trust God to reward us who diligently seek Him.

- God makes it possible for us to believe by His Holy Word, but by the human will, and individual can choose to believe or not to believe.
- An individual faith should grow in the Lord to receive His blessings.

Do You Want To See Results?

- Believe His Word
- Profess His Word
- Stand on His Word
- Receive His Word

Scriptures:

Matthew 7:16-20; 14:30-31
Romans 10:17
Ephesians 2:8
Hebrews 11:6-8
James 1:17

SESSION 3

Introducing The Study:

In this lesson, we will study how God was faithful in keeping His promises throughout the adversity in Abraham's life, Sarah's life, Joseph's life, Moses' life, and Noah's life.

♦ Abraham was justified by works in offering up Isaac, his son on the altar. "Abraham believed in the Lord and He counted it to him for righteousness." (Genesis 15:6)

♦ God put Abraham's faith to the test. He showed genuine faith by his willingness to offer up his son. His faith was a heart commitment.

- Abraham did not understand how God would keep His promises when He promised that he would be the father of many nations. He was old and had no children, but he trusted God anyway.

- Abraham knew what God had promised, and that was all that mattered to him. He knew that God would keep His promises.

- Sarah was miraculously empowered to conceived when she was past the time of life to bear a child. But, Sarah knew that God had promised her a child, and she knew that He could not go back on His Word or promises. She had faith that He would do what He had promised.

- Sarah was blessed by God to be the mother of nations, through whom the world was blessed.

- Joseph was the favored son, he was giving a beautiful robe of many colors. He forgave his brothers for doing him wrong. He recognized the ability of God to take evil and injustice to work it out for his good.

- Moses chose to leave the luxury palace of Pharaoh's and suffered hardship with God's people. Moses was a great leader when he led God's people out of bondage in Egypt.

- God blessed Noah and his sons, He said unto them, be fruitful, multiply, and replenish the earth.

We Must Apply Our Faith And Trust In The Lord:

- To receive the blessings
- To receive the promises
- To receive the victory
- To receive our healing

Scriptures:

Genesis 9:1
Genesis 12:2-3
Genesis 48:15-16
Numbers 6:22-27
Deuteronomy 33:1
Galatians 3:14-29

SESSION 4

Introducing The Study:

In this lesson, we will study how God kept the three Hebrew men when they were thrown into a fiery furnace by Nebuchadnezzar, and Daniel from the den of lions.

♦ Nebuchadnezzar, the king of Babylon, he made an idolatrous image of gold that was ninety feet high. He commanded the people to fall down to worship it when they heard the horn, flute, and all kinds of music played.

- The three faithful Hebrew men, Shadrach, Meshach, and Abednego, they refused to worship the idol and were reported by certain Chaldeans to the king.

- They were thrown into the fiery furnace that was heated seven times hotter than usual. Their confidence in deliverance stood the test.

- Nebuchadnezzar saw four men, the three Hebrew men and the Son of God. They were unharmed. The king was impressed that he forbidden anyone to speak against the God of the three Hebrew men and they were promoted in the province of Babylon.

♦ King Darius signed the written decree forbidding prayer to anyone but to him for thirty days.

- Daniel continued to pray to God, three times daily. Daniel was cast into the den of lions.

- Daniel kept the faith and was unharmed by the lions.

- King Darius issued a decree to all people, nations, and languages to honor the God of Daniel.

To Really Have Faith And Trust In God, We Are To:

- Trust in the Lord Jesus Christ with all our heart.
- Trust in the Lord Jesus Christ to direct our paths.
- Trust in the Lord Jesus Christ's strength.
- Trust in the Lord Jesus Christ to fight our battles.
- Trust in the Lord Jesus Christ to be our lawyer and judge.
- Trust in the Lord Jesus Christ to pray for us daily.
- Trust in the Lord Jesus Christ to shield us from the enemy.

How Faith In God Helps Us To Trust In Him:

- To trust in His grace
- To trust in His strength
- To trust in His protection
- To trust in His mercy
- To trust in His forgiveness
- To trust in His peace
- To trust in His love and goodness
- To trust in God always in everything, and in every circumstances.

<u>Scriptures:</u>

Daniel 1 & 2; 3:1-30
Daniel 6:1-28
Psalm 37:5
Philippians 4:6-7
1 Peter 5:7

SESSION 5

<u>Introducing The Study:</u>

In this lesson, we will study how God allowed David to be tested, and how he was a man after God's own heart.

- Satan will do everything he can to try to distract God's children from believing God and trusting in His promises. Paul was given a thorn in his flesh, the messenger of satan to buffet him, so that he can stay humbled.

- Being tested and suffering are assurance of children of God. God chastens those whom He loves.

- Suffering can cause Believers to trust and have faith in God alone instead of trusting in their strength or someone else.

- David was in distress running for his life not to get killed by Saul. He thought that he was all alone while he was in his trials. But, God was the source of all blessing for His people, Israel.

- David knew that the Lord was his strength, shield, and deliverer when he faced that giant, Goliath.

- We are to live our lives in faith, trust, hope, and love by walking under the control of the Holy Spirit.

Scriptures:

1 Samuel 13:14   Psalm 4:1
1 Samuel 17:1-45   Psalm 23
2 Samuel 5:4   Psalm 69:1-18

SESSION 6

Introducing The Study:

In this lesson, we will study how Believers can overcome the world, the flesh, and the devil. How Believers through faith are kept and guarded by the power of God.

♦ "By grace are ye saved through faith; and that not of yourself." (Ephesians 2:8-9)

♦ "Not having mine own righteousness, which is of the law, but that which is through the faith of Christ, the righteousness which is of God by faith." (Philippians 3:9)

♦ "Whosoever believeth that Jesus is the Christ is born of God: and everyone that loveth Him that begat loveth Him also that is begotten of Him. By this we know that we love the children of God, when we love God, and keep His Commandments. For this is the love of God, that we keep His Commandments are not grievous. For whatsoever is born of God overcomes the world: and this is the victory that overcomes the world, even our faith. Who is He that overcomes the world, but He that believeth that Jesus is the Son of God?" (1 John 5:1-5)

- Faithful Who promised means that everything that God promised in the New Covenant which is salvation and total victory over sin.

- We are to never stop trusting, hoping, and believing in God, it is crucial in our relationship with Him. Trust is part of having faith in God.

- Faith and trust in God will show up in our behavior, in our walk, in our talk, and daily living.

- Faith in God must also include faith in God's Son, Jesus Christ and the sacrifice He paid in full at the Cross for our sins.

- When you have faith in God, Jesus Christ, and the power of the Holy Spirit: You will not be limited in doing the work of the Lord, if you go according to His direction and instruction.

- We got to trust and obey God, even in our challenging circumstances.

- We are to live absolutely by faith, by believing, and trusting in God's Holy Word.

- We are to keep the faith in God, Jesus Christ, and what He accomplished at the Cross. Jesus Christ paid it in full at the Cross for all our sins.

- We are to look at things through the spiritual eyes of faith. We will only succeed in overcoming this world with the help of our Lord and Savior, Jesus Christ, and the Holy Spirit. Therefore, let us walk, talk, see, hear, and believe by faith in God, Jesus Christ, and the Holy Spirit.

Scriptures:

John 16:25-33
1 Corinthians 15:57
Romans 8:37

Hebrews 12:1
1 John 5:1-6

SESSION 7

Introducing The Study:

In this lesson, we will study how God tested Job's faith.

- Job was an upright, blameless, and wealthy man of God. But he was not exempt from suffering.

- Job lost his family, his possessions, his health, and his will to live.

- Job was confident that when he had been tested that he would come forth as gold.

- God had set a protective hedge around Job.

- God does not send sickness or suffering on a Believer. But God will allow a Believer to suffer to develop spiritually.

- Satan must get permission from God to try bring sickness on a Believer.

- God does not always explain the reason for Believers in suffering. But suffering develops endurance and perseverance.

Ephesians 3:17-20

(v.17) "That Christ may dwell in your hearts by faith; that ye, being rooted and grounded in love."

(v.18) "May be able to comprehend with all saints what is the breath, length, depth, and height."

(v.19) "To know the love of Christ, which passeth knowledge, that ye might be filled with all the fulness of God."

(v.20) "Now unto Him that is able to do exceeding abundantly above all that we ask or think, according to the power that worketh in us."

- The light affliction is but for a moment, the affliction refers to the hardships, trials, and sufferings in which the world has to offer. But the glory is eternal and the reward that awaits the faithful servant of Christ Jesus at the Judgment Seat of God.

- God does not promise us deliverance from persecution, but deliverance through the persecution if we trust Him.

- When life seems unfair, and you are depressed about life's situations, remember that God loves you and He will see you through if you have placed your faith and trust in Him.

<u>Scriptures:</u>

Job 1:1-22; 3:1-11
Job 11:1-15
James 1:12-15

SESSION 8

Introducing The Study:

In this lesson, we will study how Christians can make a stand in their faith in any circumstances.

1 Peter 5:9

"Whom resist steadfast in the faith, knowing that the same afflictions are accomplished in your brethren that are in the world."

- Faith in God and Jesus Christ, and what He accomplished at the Cross. Jesus Christ is the source of everything.

- The Cross is the mean for everything and the Holy Spirit over sees it all when you place your faith in Jesus Christ.

- Faith is the key that unlocks the door and causes God to move on your behalf. Therefore, turn that key and live the life that God has for you to live and be free from bondage. If you place your faith in everything else and the law, it will put you back in bondage, the law condemned, but grace forgives."

- Faith in God will see us through any circumstances, situations, or obstacles. God has an appointed time for His work to be accomplished. He will be sure to do the work when the time comes. We are to wait on His time, and not anticipate His appointed time. We are to wait patiently upon Him. We shall not be anxious or disappointed in it. He will fully answer our prayers in what we are believing and having faith in Him to do according to His will.

- When we pray for something according to God's Will, we must have the faith to know that He will answer our prayers. We must observe what answers He gives us by His Word and the Holy Spirit.

♦ "The vision is yet for an appointed time to come." (Habakkuk 2:3)

Scriptures:

Matthew 9:29
Matthew 24:13
Mark 11:24
Luke 17:33
2 Corinthians 1:24

SESSION 9

Introducing The Study:

In this lesson, we will study how Christians should withstand the test, trials, and storms of life. How God gives Christians the support or relief to sustain in their faith.

- Maintaining your faith in God through difficulties can be very hard. But if we keep our faith, trust, and hope in God during the hard times. He will give us peace during the midst of the storm.

- Faith in God gives us strength, peace, joy, and hope for today, tomorrow, and the future.

- Perseverance in the faith by enduring hardships even when life seems unbearable and the pressure is on.

- When we rely and rest on the Lord, He gives us peace. We won't get frustrated, we won't get burn out, and we won't struggle when we rest in the Lord and what He accomplished at the Cross.

- If you have placed your faith in God and keep His Commandments. You will live a victorious life. You will be blessed today, tomorrow, and forever.

- If you disobey Him, you can cause curses upon yourself.

- You must continue to believe and to profess that you are still standing your ground in the Lord even though the things you desired in prayer haven't manifested yet. You must tell the devil that he is a liar and that you believe in the Lord and His Word.

- God knows and understands your problems, so cast your cares up on Him and be deliverance.

<u>Scriptures:</u>

Isaiah 40:28-31
2 Corinthians 4:16-18
1Timothy 1:19; 4:12
Hebrews 11:13
James 1:6-7
1 John 5:13

SESSION 10

<u>Introducing The Study:</u>

In this lesson, we will study how Christians must stay faithful even until the end in order to receive the blessings from the Lord.

- We should keep on growing in the Lord and bearing good fruits of the Lord until Jesus Christ returns.

- We should want to be faithful till the end, be ready at all time, without spot or blemish.

- Jesus died on the Cross for our sins, but we must accept salvation by faith in the Lord and what He did on the Cross at Calvary.

- Jesus provided a way for us to have a relationship with God, and to be with Him forever.

- The enemy, the devil tries to torment you with fear, doubt, and worries to lure you away from God. But no matter what, you must stand on God's Holy Word, keep the faith, and trust Him that He is still at work in your life and that He keeps His promises.

- Jesus' teaching about a tiny mustard seed, is just like a small amount of faith. This is to remind us that we must trust God and put our faith into action daily.

- When fear, doubt, worries, unforgiveness, or deception knocks at the door of your heart, you must allow faith to respond. We are to be persistent by responding with a heart full of faith, and walk in the authority over the enemy, the devil.

- If we stand on His Holy Word and keep His Commandments, we will see the victory.

<u>Scriptures</u>:

Psalm 1:1-2
Psalm 31:23-24
1 Corinthians 1:9
Philippians 1:6
1 Thessalonians 1:3
2 Thessalonians 3:3
1 John 1:9

ABOUT THE AUTHOR

Elder Lisa Driver-Crummy resides in North Carolina with her family. Reuben and Lisa are the proud parent of a brilliant son, Reubeneeco, and two beautiful daughters, Victoria and Alessia. Lisa earned a Master's Degree in Adult Education from AIU. Lisa graduated from UAB in 1990 with a B.S. in Education and a minor in Sociology. She graduated from the New Covenant Bible Institute, Inc., with a Bachelor of Theology.

Lisa is an Ordained Minister, Evangelist, Teacher, Mentor, and an Author. She has done several speaking engagements and workshops. She is the founder of LRC4HisKingdomMinistries. Lisa has learned how to put all her faith and trust in the Lord, rely on the Holy Spirit, and believe in God's Holy Word. She is inspired to express the goodness of the Lord and to encourage others through her writing. Lisa thanks God for giving her the victory through all her trials and tribulations. She was tested by her faith in the Lord, when the enemy tried to put breast cancer on her. She stood on God's Holy Word and believed God for her healing. She was hit by a big dumped trunk, couldn't get out of her vehicle, and was rushed to the emergency. She is very grateful for the Lord saving her. She thanks God for the Holy Spirit leading and guiding her through her faith walk in life. Her faith and trust are in God the Father, God the Son (Jesus Christ), and God the Holy Spirit forever! She blesses His Holy Name (Lord Jesus Christ) forevermore!

ABOUT THE AUTHOR

Rev. Belinda Driver-McCain resides in Alabama with her family. She has been married to her husband, Roosevelt McCain for 38 years. She has two children, Roosevelt McCain Jr. and Roshanda McCain. She has two brilliant granddaughters Paige and Libertee. She has a grandson, Kevin. She is an Ordained Elder Ordained Pastor, has been an ordained elder since 2000, and a Licensed Minister since 1996. She has served as president of the Women Aglow Ministries. She was the guest speaker of Morning Inspiration WYAM Ch. 56 and Ch. 23 in Decatur/Jasper, AL host. She has traveled to several states to preach the Word God as a motivator guest speaker. She served as a facilitator, guest speaker, teacher in several states, including in Jerusalem, Israel. She has a Master's Degree in Christian Education from Birmingham Theology Seminary in Birmingham, AL. She earned a B.S. in Health Administration at UAB, Birmingham, AL. She earned a degree in Nursing. She is a Pastor, Prophet, Evangelist, Mentor, and an Author. She is the founder of Kingdom Builder Ministries.

Belinda's Testimony

"Hallelujah! Hallelujah! Hallelujah! Look what the Lord has done. In 2017, Belinda was dying just a little over a year ago. She could feel her spirit leaving her body when she had a hip replacement done. She was operated on three times in less than two weeks from having her hip replacement. She had to stay in the hospital and nursing home for over three months with a pic line running through her heart, was on antibiotic for over two months and was totally bedridden. She couldn't walk for two years. She had another hip replacement this year, but she is now walking with a walker. She thanks the Lord Jesus Christ for bring her through her sickness and blessing her to be able to walk. She is believing God that soon she will be able to walk with the cane. Hallelujah! Praise the Lord!

For I know who I am and to Whom I belong to, I am a part of a fellowship of the unashamed. I am a committed Believer; a disciple of Jesus Christ and I won't look back; let up; or give up. I will stay stored up; prayed up; paid up; and spoken up for the cause of Jesus Christ. I am a satisfied bond servant of the Lord Jesus Christ. Am I not free? Am I not an Apostle? Have I not seen Jesus our Lord? Because of the finished work of Jesus Christ, my delivered from death, where the devil thought he had me, but my Jesus came and rescued me. Hallelujah! The Lord has always had His hands on me every since I was a child. The devil has tried to kill me every since I was a child. I remember taking a full bottle of aspirin when I was about five years of age. I almost drown in a lake. I was delivered by the hands of God, when I tried to commit several suicidal attempts. I was smashed between two cars when I was very small. The Lord healed me from pancreatic disease. If the devil would have had his way, I would be dead today. He knew that God had great work for me to do."

Uplifting Spirit Filled Support Nuggets:

"Stay calm Jesus Christ is our Healer and Deliverer!"

"Stay calm Jesus Christ is coming back soon!"

"Stay calm and breathe, God got this!"

"With God's help, we can run this race!"

SIT "Stepping Into Faith"

FIG "Faith In God"

GIB "God Is Bigger"

L4J "Living For Jesus"

FITLJC "Faith In The Lord Jesus Christ!"

TYLJC "Thank You Lord Jesus Christ!"

WWJS "What Will Jesus Say?"
WDJS "What Did Jesus Say?"
J4MP "Joy for my pain"

#More Lord
#More Obedience
#More Victory
#Less Me

#More Jesus Christ
#More Love
#More Peace
#More Happiness

#Put actions with your faith!

#Faith stops doubt in its tracks!

#Big in knowledge
#Big in Wisdom
#Big in Prayer
#Big in God

#I'm happy in Jesus Christ!

#Living life God's way, not man!
#Be you and no one else!
#No time to faint, hold on to your faith!
#I just thank Jesus Christ!
#Living large and the good life in Jesus Christ!

#Don't sweat the small things, be content in Jesus!
#Rise higher in Jesus!
#Whatever you need, it is in Jesus Christ!
#God is in control, just praise Him!
#Live from within your heart, not your mind!

OTHER BOOKS TO READ

"Break Yourself Free from Bondage"

"By His Spirit"

"My Courageous Princess"

FIG

FAITH IN GOD

Printed in the United States
By Bookmasters